HISTORY
⋆ V·I·P ⋆

MARY ANNING

BRILLIANT
BIOGRAPHIES
of the
DEAD FAMOUS

First published in paperback in 2016 by Wayland

Editor: Annabel Stones
Designer: Rocket Design (East Anglia) Ltd
Illustration: Emmanuel Cerisier, Beehive Illustration
Proofreader: Rebecca Clunes

Dewey number: 560.9'2-dc23
ISBN   978 0 7502 9914 5
Library ebook ISBN: 9780750288521
10 9 8 7 6 5 4 3 2 1

Wayland

An imprint of

Hachette Children's Group

Part of Hodder & Stoughton

Carmelite House

50 Victoria Embankment

London EC4Y 0DZ

An Hachette UK Company

www.hachette.co.uk

www.hachettechildrens.co.uk

Printed in China

Picture credits: iStock: p.6 © GeorgiosArt, p.11 © traveler1116, p.21 top © Matt84; Science & Society Picture Library: p.26 © National Media Museum; Science Picture Library: p.4 Natural History Museum, London, p.21 bottom Natural History Museum, London, p.25 Paul D Stewart, p.28 Natural History Museum, London; Shutterstock: p.7 Teguh Mujiono, p.9 top Gail Johnson, p.9 bottom Pitamaha, p.15 IgorGolovniov, p.18 Lefteris Papaulakis, p.22 IgorGolovniov, p.29 Nicku; Wikimedia Commons: p.17 CC Ballista at English Wikipedia.
All graphic elements: Shutterstock.

2

CONTENTS

Introducing
MARY ANNING

If you thought fossil hunters were all top palaeontologists, then think again. The 'greatest fossilist the world ever knew', according to *The British Journal for the History of Science*, was a poor woman who barely went to school. She was born over two centuries ago in the small English coastal town of Lyme Regis, where she spent her life discovering fossil treasure. Her name was Mary Anning.

> She sells seashells on the seashore.
> The shells she sells are seashells, I'm sure.
> For if she sells seashells on the seashore
> Then I'm sure she sells seashore shells.
>
> Terry Sullivan (1908)

WELL I NEVER!

Many say that the tongue twister 'She sells seashells' is actually about Anning, who sold fossils from a stall on the Lyme Regis seafront.

Mary Anning lived during the nineteenth century, which was not a good time for women to study palaeontology – the science of fossil animals and plants. Some thought that women weren't clever enough to understand the subject. Women were not allowed to join the Geological Society of London until the twentieth century. They couldn't even go to the Society's lectures, where fossil finds were discussed.

Anning didn't start out as a palaeontologist. She simply hunted for fossils along the shorelines to the east and west of her seaside home. She sold the fossils that she found to tourists and collectors. As well as being a source of income for Mary and her family, these fossils would become hugely important in another way… They changed the study of prehistoric life for ever.

WHO WAS SHE?

FULL NAME: Mary Anning

DATE OF BIRTH: 21 May 1799

LIVED: Lyme Regis, Dorset, England

PARENTS: Richard and Mary (known as Molly)

SIBLINGS: 9 (8 died in childhood)

JOB: Fossilist and palaeontologist

MARRIED: No

CHILDREN: No

DIED: 9 March 1847

BESIDE _the_ SEASIDE

Anning was born and lived in Lyme Regis on the south coast of England. At the end of the eighteenth century, the small seaside town was already famous for the fossils that peppered its cliffs and beaches. But no one knew what the fossils were or why they were there. They were nicknamed 'curiosities' because people were so curious about these strange objects.

IN OTHER NEWS

In the late eighteenth century, Lyme Regis became a top holiday spot for the well off. New roads made it easier to travel there and sea bathing was the latest craze. Regency author Jane Austen visited Lyme Regis with her family in 1803 and 1804. She liked it so much that the town features in her last novel – _Persuasion_ (1818).

Anning's father, Richard Anning, worked as a carpenter and cabinet-maker but was also a keen fossil hunter. This wasn't just a hobby. The Anning family was desperately poor and by selling the fossils he found, Richard could make extra money to support them.

Fossil hunting was a skill that Richard taught his children. At low tide, he took Mary and her brother Joseph to the shoreline, showing them how to spot spiral-shaped ammonites and smooth, pointed belemnites. They learned how to clean the fossils to get them ready to sell.

The Annings sold their fossil finds from a stall on the Lyme Regis seafront. Their customers were the wealthy tourists who visited the seaside town in summer.

★ Fossils ★

A fossil is the remains or imprint of a prehistoric animal or plant found in rocks. The Annings found fossils in sedimentary rocks, which were formed on the seabed millions of years ago.

When creatures died, they were covered by sediment – sand, mud and small rocks. Over many years, the sediment was pressed down under more and more layers of sediment, and eventually they all became rock. The creatures' remains trapped inside the rock were also squeezed until they became fossils, which are almost like rock themselves. The reason most fossils are of bones, teeth and shells is that the soft parts of the creatures often rotted away before the sediment buried them.

FOSSILS, FOSSILS, *everywhere*

For a fossil hunter, Lyme Regis is one of the best places in the world. It sits in the middle of a coastline that contains countless fossils. Every time a little more of the cliffs crumble away, they reveal yet more creatures from prehistoric times. When she began fossil hunting, Anning was simply looking for 'curiosities' to sell. She probably had no idea that the fossils she found were about 200 million years old.

TRUE or FALSE?

IT'S ILLEGAL TO TAKE ANY FOSSIL HOME.

false Fossil hunters are allowed to take their finds away with them. But there are rules to make sure that fossil hunters stay safe and fossils are collected responsibly. If you go fossil hunting, check the National Fossil Collecting Code before you set off and remember that any really special finds should be shown to a museum.

Scientists now know that the area around Lyme Regis was once covered with shallow seas full of sea creatures and swimming reptiles. This is why many of the fossils Anning found belonged to sea creatures.

Top spots for fossil hunting were the cliffs around Lyme Regis and nearby Charmouth. The cliffs here are a rock formation made up of layers of limestone and clay, known as Blue Lias. This rock formed on the seabed, but over millions of years, the landscape has slowly changed and moved so that some is now above water level. Coastal erosion and landslips reveal fossils preserved by these rocks.

★ The ★ Jurassic Coast

Lyme Regis is part of the Jurassic Coast — the name given to 153km of dramatic coastline that stretches from East Devon to Dorset. Here, visitors can see layers of rock that date back to the Cretaceous (65–145 million years ago), Jurassic (145–200 million years ago) and the Triassic (200–250 million years ago) periods.

The rocks here are 140 million years old.

BLEAK TIMES

When Anning was eleven, tragedy struck. Her father was suffering from a disease called tuberculosis. Then one day, he fell from a cliff. Richard Anning was already so weak from his illness that he did not recover from the accident. He died in 1810, aged just 44. It was yet another sad event for the family. Anning's elder sister – also called Mary – had died in a house fire when she was just four.

TRUE or FALSE?

MARY ANNING WAS ONCE STRUCK BY LIGHTNING.

true It happened when Anning was just a year old. While she was watching a travelling show with a neighbour, a storm blew up and they sheltered under a tree with two other women. When lightning struck, Anning was the only survivor. Once a poorly baby, it is said that after the storm, she was so lively and curious and bright that people decided that it must be because of the lightning bolt...

In all, eight of Anning's nine brothers and sisters would die in childhood. Unfortunately, this was not at all unusual. At the beginning of the nineteenth century, half of all children never reached the age of five.

For a poor family such as the Annings, life was difficult. Food shortages and poor harvests made things worse. Wheat prices rocketed and so did the cost of bread, which meant that poor people like the Annings could hardly afford to eat. It's said that Richard Anning himself protested against food shortages.

When Richard Anning died, life became even more difficult for the family. They were already poor, but he had left them in terrible debt too. Now that the earnings he'd once made from his carpentry had vanished, fossil hunting was more important then ever before.

IN OTHER NEWS

WAR! When Anning was born, the French Revolutionary Wars were raging around the world and the Napoleonic Wars were just about to begin.

During the wars, both British and French navies blockaded ports in the English Channel, which meant that it was difficult to import or export food.

BACK to the BEACH

After their father's death, Mary and Joseph Anning returned to the shoreline looking for fossils to sell. They had stiff competition because they weren't the only fossil hunters in Lyme Regis.

Other locals found and sold fossils to wealthy tourists as well. Luckily, there were plenty of ammonite and belemnite fossils for everyone to find.

WELL I NEVER!

West of Lyme Regis on Monmouth Beach, there is a real treat for fossil hunters — the Ammonite Pavement. Here, hundreds of ammonite fossils lie side by side, frozen in time.

Ammonites had once been sea creatures with ribbed, spiral shells. They were around for hundreds of millions of years before becoming extinct at the same time as the dinosaurs. Belemnite fossils were the remains of sea creatures similar to squid and cuttlefish today. They had ten arms and an ink sac and lived in a long, pointy shell.

But ammonites and belemnites were common, so the Annings needed to find a rare fossil if they wanted to stand out from the crowd. Something really special could make them a lot of money.

TRUE or FALSE?

ANNING DISCOVERED PREHISTORIC INK.

true In 1826, Anning found a belemnite fossil with dried ink inside. Her friend Elizabeth Philpot added water to the prehistoric ink and used it to draw … fossils!

★ A fellow ★ collector

Elizabeth Philpot (1780–1857) was a fossil collector who moved from London to Lyme Regis in 1805. Even though she was much older and richer than Anning, they became good friends because of their shared interest in fossils. They often went fossil hunting together. Elizabeth Philpot's fish-fossil collection is very important in its own right and is now kept at Oxford University Museum in the UK.

an IMPORTANT DISCOVERY

In 1811, Joseph Anning struck fossil gold when he found a large skull with a long jaw and large eye sockets. At first, people thought the fossil must have belonged to a crocodile, even though there were big differences. Mary Anning did not discover the skull herself, but she did spend the next year uncovering the rest of the creature's skeleton. Together, the two finds added up to one of the most important discoveries ever made in the study of natural history.

The find was the first complete skeleton of a marine reptile. The creature had lived millions of years ago, long before crocodiles even existed.

The new creature needed a name. Geologists and palaeontologists Henry de la Beche – a friend of Anning's – and William Conybeare saw that its skeleton was like a reptile, but it also looked like a fish. So they named it 'fish lizard' or 'ichthyosaur' in Greek.

The Annings' ichthyosaur fossil made a huge difference to what people knew of the history of the Earth. Until then it had been popularly believed that the Earth was only 6,000 years old and that it and the creatures who lived on it were exactly the same as the day the planet was created. Now, long-dead creatures had been found preserved inside very old rocks. This showed that not only had living creatures changed, so had the planet.

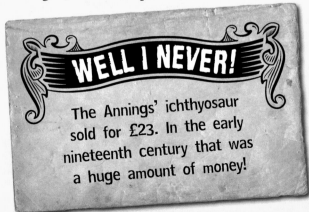

WELL I NEVER!

The Annings' ichthyosaur sold for £23. In the early nineteenth century that was a huge amount of money!

IMPORTANT FIND

ICHTHYOSAUR

Species found by the Annings:
temnodontosaurus platyodon

Also known as: fish lizard

Type of creature: predatory
marine reptile

Lived: about 250–90 million
years ago

Size: about 2 to 4m – though
some were much longer

Description:
huge eyes; long, thin nose;
many teeth; short neck;
paddles; tail fin

Sketch of an ichthyosaur skull

THE DANGERS of FOSSIL HUNTING

Anning's job was far from easy. She walked the beaches in all weathers, searching for the fossils that would support her family. As well as being hard work, fossil hunting could be dangerous. If she were caught by the rising tide, she might drown. And the Blue Lias cliffs were notoriously unstable...

By far the best time to look for fossils was during the winter, when the weather was worst. Stormy seas lashed the shoreline, while heavy rain caused landslides. As the cliffs crumbled away, new fossils were revealed. It was at this moment that the cliffs were also at their most unstable. More landslides could happen at any moment.

But fossils meant money, and by this time Anning had built up a reputation for herself and collectors were eager to buy her next finds. To find fossils before anyone else, landslides were a risk she had to take.

In 1833, it was very nearly the end for Anning when she narrowly avoided being killed by falling rocks. She survived, but her terrier, Tray, who trekked the beaches with her, was crushed. Anning was devastated to lose her faithful dog.

TRUE or FALSE?

JOSEPH ANNING GAVE UP FOSSIL HUNTING TO MAKE CURTAINS.

false Joseph did give up fossil hunting in the 1820s, but it was to take up an apprenticeship as a furniture upholsterer. From then on, Mary was in charge of the family business, though her mother helped out by making deals with fossil collectors and palaeontologists.

IN OTHER NEWS

"[Anning] has for years gone daily in search of fossil remains of importance at every tide, for many miles under the hanging cliffs at Lyme, whose fallen masses are her immediate object, as they alone contain these valuable relics of a former world…"

The Bristol Mirror, 1823

PALAEONTOLOGY for BEGINNERS

The only school Anning ever went to was Sunday school – and she didn't go there often – so she was never taught to read and write. Science was just one of many subjects that she knew nothing about. If she wanted to learn more about the fossils she found, she had to get an education.

Anning did learn how to read and write – by teaching herself. Now, she could make notes about what she'd found. She drew detailed diagrams recording exactly what her fossils looked like. Anning also read everything she could about fossil discoveries that had been made so far, often copying important papers to keep for herself.

Without knowing it, Anning had begun to study a type of science that was still very new – palaeontology. As well as being a fossil hunter and a fossil dealer, she was now learning to be a palaeontologist too.

TRUE or FALSE?

BRONTOSAURUS WAS A HUGE PLANT-EATING DINOSAUR THAT LIVED DURING THE JURASSIC PERIOD.

undecided The name Brontosaurus was given to a dinosaur skeleton found by a palaeontologist. Later, other scientists decided it was actually a type of Apatosaurus – which had already been discovered. But, some palaeontologists now think that Brontosaurus might be a separate kind of dinosaur, after all!

Brontosaurus was actually Apatosaurus all along... or was it?

Soon, Anning could recognise fossilised bones when she found them and often knew which animal they had belonged to. As her knowledge grew, she also knew exactly where these fitted in a creature's skeleton. Whenever she had enough pieces, she rebuilt the skeleton herself and fixed the bones in cement.

IN OTHER NEWS

One rich fossil collector was worried about the Annings – who despite the sale of the ichthyosaur and many other fossils were still very poor. So, he decided to do something about it. In 1820, Lieutenant-Colonel Birch auctioned his fossil collection and sent the money to Anning and her family. Perhaps Birch felt a little guilty. The auction made £400, which was almost certainly a lot more money than Birch paid when he first bought the fossils from the Annings.

the NEXT BIG THING

Years went by and Anning continued to scour the Jurassic Coast for fossils. She found plenty more ichthyosaurs, but none created as much excitement as the first find until the fossil she unearthed in 1820. It was another sea creature – one with a very long neck. But what made this fossil really special was that it was the first of its kind – a brand new creature!

IMPORTANT FIND

PLESIOSAUR

Species found by Anning: *plesiosaurus dolichodeirus*

Also known as: *near lizard*

Type of creature: *predatory marine reptile*

Lived: *about 205–66 million years ago*

Size: *about 5m long*

Speed: *about 8kph*

Description: *flat, wide body; four flippers; short tail; long neck (though some plesiosaurs had short necks).*

A palaeontologist called William Conybeare gave the creature a proper name: plesiosaur. This means 'near lizard'. However, there was one very important thing missing from the fossil — a skull. Without it, experts didn't know exactly what the creature looked like. But in 1823, Anning solved the problem when she found another plesiosaur, this time with a skull.

Conybeare described the prehistoric creature to the Geological Society of London in 1824. But he forgot to give members of the society one vital detail about the find: he didn't tell them that Anning had found it.

TRUE *or* FALSE?

THE LOCH NESS MONSTER WAS ACTUALLY A PLESIOSAUR.

false There's no proof that the Loch Ness monster ever existed, but if it had then it and the long-necked plesiosaur were alike. They were both scary swimming creatures with exceedingly long necks. But there's a really big reason why they could not be the same creature. Plesiosaurs became extinct at the same time as the dinosaurs 65 million years ago, while Loch Ness, supposedly the mythical monster's home, is just 10,000 years old.

Anning's letter and drawing that announced the discovery of the plesiosaur.

ALMOST FAMOUS

Despite the fact that her discoveries weren't officially recognised – something that upset her – Anning's reputation as a fossil hunter and palaeontologist was growing. The general public hadn't yet heard of her, but in scientific circles her name was becoming well known. By now, she had found and examined so many fossils that she often knew more than the experts.

In 1824, Anning shared her theory about fossils known as 'bezoar stones'. She had noticed that some weirdly shaped fossils were usually found near a creature's stomach. When she looked inside them, she discovered that they contained tiny remnants of other animals. Anning thought that these fossils might not be bones at all, but were actually prehistoric poo. She was right. Ideas like this proved to the scientific community, that Anning was worth listening to.

Sketch of a 'bezoar stone'

~ PTEROSAUR ~

Species found by Anning:
dimorphodon macronyx

Also known as: *two-form tooth*

Type of creature: *flying reptile*

Lived: *about 205–66 million years ago*

Size: *its wingspan was nearly 1.5m wide*

Speed: *unknown*

Description:
large head, pointed teeth, large claws, long tail, large wings

Then, in 1828, she made another discovery that boosted her reputation among scientists further. She found a pterosaur – a kind of prehistoric flying reptile. It was the first fossil of its kind to be found in the UK.

WHAT THEY SAID

[Anning] has made herself so thoroughly acquainted with the science that the moment she finds any bones she knows to what tribe they belong ... by reading and application she has arrived to that degree of knowledge as to be in the habit of writing and talking with professors and other clever men on the subject, and they all acknowledge that she understands more of the science than anyone else in this kingdom.

Lady Harriet Silvester, who visited Anning in 1824

FOSSILIST FRIENDS

In the nineteenth century, many thought women were not clever enough to understand science. They weren't allowed to go to university or to join scientific societies. The women who did manage to study usually had one thing in common – they were rich.

They had the freedom to learn because they didn't have to spend time earning money to support themselves. Anning was a poor woman. How could she hope to join in?

WHAT THEY SAID

She says the world has used her ill... these men of learning have sucked her brains, and made a great deal of publishing works, of which she furnished the contents, while she derived none of the advantages.

Anna Pinney, a friend of Anning (nineteenth century)

Even though Anning only left Lyme Regis once in her lifetime – when she made a short trip to London – she did meet fellow scientists. They heard of her impressive discoveries and vast knowledge of fossils and came to see her. From her friends Henry de la Beche (shown opposite) and William Buckland to famous palaeontologist William Conybeare, Anning wasn't short of visitors. They came to hunt fossils with her, to see her latest finds and to talk with her too.

A meeting with Gideon Mantell even inspired him to look for and find his very own dinosaur – the iguanodon.

Still, it saddened Anning to think that she helped so many others to study palaeontology, yet was hardly ever given the credit she deserved. She was virtually unknown to anyone who wasn't a scientist.

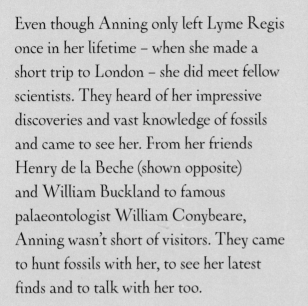

Gideon Mantell and his iguanodon

IN OTHER NEWS

In the nineteenth century, Charlotte, Emily and Anne Brontë published books under the names Currer, Ellis and Acton Bell to disguise the fact that they were actually women. They worried that readers wouldn't take them seriously otherwise.

THE END of AN ERA

In 1835, a bad investment meant that Anning lost most of the money she'd saved. She was poor once more – how would she survive? Thankfully, the scientific community came to her rescue.

With the support of the British government, Anning was given a pension in recognition of her huge contributions to science and geology. Later, she became the first honorary member of Dorset County Museum.

Historians think this very early photograph may be the only one ever taken of Mary Anning. It dates back to 1843 and is called 'The Geologists'.

IN OTHER NEWS

TWO KINGS, A QUEEN AND A PRINCE REGENT

Even though Anning died when she was just 47, she lived to see four British monarchs. These were King George III, the Prince Regent (later King George IV), William IV and Queen Victoria – who reigned from 1837 to 1901. It wasn't until three years after Victoria's death that women were allowed to become members of the Geological Society of London, at last.

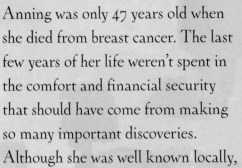

Anning was only 47 years old when she died from breast cancer. The last few years of her life weren't spent in the comfort and financial security that should have come from making so many important discoveries. Although she was well known locally, most of the general public did not know of her achievements.

By the time of her death, however, Anning was such an important figure in the world of science that the president of the Geological Society of London spoke at her funeral in Lyme Regis. The president was her old friend, Henry de la Beche.

WHAT THEY SAID

This window is sacred to the memory of Mary Anning of this parish, who died 9 March 1847 and is erected by the vicar and some members of the Geological Society of London in commemoration of her usefulness in furthering the science of geology, as also of her benevolence of heart and integrity of life.

Inscription beneath the stained-glass window in Mary Anning's local church.

FAME at LAST

Anning discovered prehistoric creatures that wowed the world. She helped to show that our planet is a very old place indeed. Meanwhile, the contributions she made to the study of palaeontology are beyond measure. Now, over two hundred years after she was born, Mary Anning has at last achieved the fame she deserved.

PLESIOSAURUS MACROCEPHALUS.

TRUE or FALSE?

GOOGLE CELEBRATED ANNING'S 215TH BIRTHDAY.

true The search engine marked 21 May 2014 on their homepage with a picture of Mary Anning finding the fossil of a prehistoric reptile.

While Anning was alive, she wasn't properly credited for her discoveries – that honour went to the men who'd bought the fossils from her. Today, her portrait is proudly displayed in the Natural History Museum in London. Some of her most important finds are nearby in the Fossil Marine Reptile Gallery, including the famous ichthyosaur that she and her brother found. It's thanks to her that people began to realise that Earth and life on it hadn't always stayed exactly the same.

In 2010, the Royal Society of London named the ten most important British women in the history of science – and Mary Anning was one of them. In 2015, palaeontologists discovered that a fossil found on the Jurassic Coast in the 1980s was actually a brand new species of ichthyosaur. It was named *ichthyosaurus anning* after Mary Anning.

TOP TEN

The ten most influential British women in the history of science.

Caroline Herschel (1750–1848) Astronomer

Mary Somerville (1780–1872) Scientist and mathematician

Mary Anning (1799–1847) Palaeontologist

Elizabeth Garrett Anderson (1836–1917) Physician and surgeon

Hertha Ayrton (1854–1923) Engineer, mathematician and physicist

Kathleen Lonsdale (1903–1971) Physicist and crystallographer

Elsie Widdowson (1908–2000) Dietician

Dorothy Hodgkin (1910–1994) Biochemist and crystallographer

Rosalind Franklin (1920–1958) Chemist and crystallographer

Anne McLaren (1927–2007) Biologist

THE ROYAL SOCIETY (2010)

WHAT THEY SAID

Her history shows what humble people may do, if they have just purpose and courage enough, toward promoting the cause of science. The carpenter's daughter has won a name for herself, and has deserved to win it.

Charles Dickens (1865)

1796 Joseph Anning (Mary's brother) is born.

1799 Mary Anning is born.

1800 She is struck by lightning.

1803 Jane Austen first visits Lyme Regis.

1805 Elizabeth Philpot moves to Lyme Regis.

1810 Richard Anning (Mary's father) dies.

1811 Joseph Anning finds an ichthyosaur skull.

1812 Mary Anning finds the rest of the ichthyosaur's skeleton. Later, it is named the *temnodontosaurus platyodon*.

1820 Lieutenant-Colonel Birch auctions the fossils he bought from the Annings and gives them the proceeds.

1820 Mary Anning finds a plesiosaur without a skull.

1823 She discovers the *plesiosaurus dolichodeirus*.

1824 She shares the theory that bezoar stones are really prehistoric poo.

1826 She opens her shop – Anning's Fossil Depot.

1828 She finds a pterosaur, later named the *dimorphodon macronyx*.

1833 She is nearly killed in a landslide.

1835 She loses a lot of money.

1847 Mary Anning dies.

2010 Royal Society names Anning as one of the most important women in science.

Prehistory

200 million years ago
At the beginning of the Jurassic period, Lyme Regis is covered by shallow seas, in which prehistoric marine reptiles swim and sea creatures live.

66 million years ago
An asteroid hits the Yucatán Peninsula in Mexico, causing the extinction of many species of prehistoric creatures around the world.

GLOSSARY

acquaint to get to know someone or something

ammonite prehistoric sea creature with a ribbed, spiral shell

apprenticeship working and learning a trade at the same time

auction a public sale where things are sold to whoever promises to pay the highest price

belemnite prehistoric sea creature very like a squid or cuttlefish

benevolence kindness

contribution the act of giving something

debt owing money

erosion when something is worn away by water or wind

extinction when a species dies out completely

fossil the remains of a plant or animal, preserved as a shape or a mould in rock

fossilist someone who collects and studies fossils

geologist an expert in geology, which is the study of the earth

integrity honesty

landslide when earth or rock slides down a cliff or mountain

marine found in the sea

natural history the scientific study of animals and plants

palaeontology the science of fossil animals and plants

plesiosaur predatory marine reptile

predatory when an animal hunts other animals to survive

prehistoric a time so long ago that it was before records were kept

promote make something better

pterosaur flying reptile

Regency to do with the late eighteenth and early nineteenth centuries

relic something special that has survived from long ago

theory an idea

tuberculosis a disease that affects the lungs

upholsterer someone who fits padded coverings to furniture such as sofas and armchairs

further information

BOOKS

The Fossil Girl by Catherine Brighton (Frances Lincoln Children's Books, 2006)

The Official Guide to the Jurassic Coast by Denys Brunsden (Coastal Publishing, 2003)

DK Eyewitness: Rock and Fossil Hunter by Ben Morgan (Dorling Kindersley, 2015)

WEBSITES

www.nhm.ac.uk/nature-online/science-of-natural-history/biographies/mary-anning/
The Natural History Museum's biography and timeline of Mary Anning.

www.lymeregismuseum.co.uk/in-the-museum/mary-anning
Lyme Regis Museum's biography about Mary Anning.

www.bbc.co.uk/schools/primaryhistory/famouspeople/mary_anning/
Information, photos, videos, a quiz and more fun activities.

PLACES TO VISIT

The Natural History Museum, Cromwell Road, London, SW7 5BD

Lyme Regis Museum, Bridge Street, Lyme Regis, Dorset, DT7 3QA

Oxford University Museum of Natural History, Parks Road, Oxford, OX1 3PW

INDEX